D1282760

SOLVING REAL-WORLD PROBLEMS WITH CIVIL ENGINEERING

THERESE SHEA

Britannica
Educational Publishing

IN ASSOCIATION WITH

ROSEN
EDUCATIONAL SERVICES

Published in 2016 by Britannica Educational Publishing (a trademark of Encyclopædia Britannica, Inc.) in association with The Rosen Publishing Group, Inc.
29 East 21st Street, New York, NY 10010

Distributed exclusively by Rosen Publishing.
To see additional Britannica Educational Publishing titles, go to rosenpublishing.com.

First Edition

Britannica Educational Publishing
J.E. Luebering: Director, Core Reference Group
Mary Rose McCudden: Editor, Britannica Student Encyclopedia

Rosen Publishing
Christine Poolos: Editor
Nelson Sá: Art Director
Michael Moy: Designer
Cindy Reiman: Photography Manager
Rona Tucciillo: Photo Researcher

Library of Congress Cataloging-in-Publication Data

Shea, Therese, author.
Solving real-world problems with civil engineering / Therese Shea. — First edition.
    pages cm. — (Let's find out! Engineering)
Audience: Grades 1 to 4.
Includes bibliographical references and index.3#
ISBN 978-1-68048-260-7 (library bound) — ISBN 978-1-5081-0067-6 (pbk.) — ISBN 978-1-68048-318-5 (6-pack)
1. Civil engineering—Juvenile literature. I. Title.
TA149.S54 2016
624—dc23

2015014582

Manufactured in the United States of America

CONTENTS

ENGINEERING 101

Engineering is using science and math as well as knowledge of forces of nature to figure out how to solve problems. Engineers are involved in the many steps of creating problem-solving structures, products, and processes. They come up with an idea, they design it, they create it, and then they make sure it works to

Engineers may work with architects, a construction crew, and other people at a job site.

To **design** means to think up or plan something for a purpose.

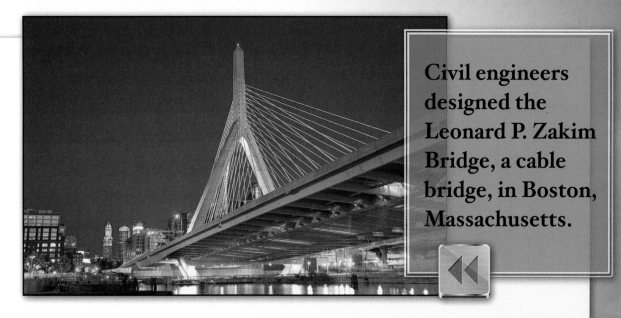

Civil engineers designed the Leonard P. Zakim Bridge, a cable bridge, in Boston, Massachusetts.

fix the problem. Engineers also fix or improve existing structures, products, and processes.

Different kinds of engineers solve different problems. However, an engineer working in one field usually requires some knowledge of other fields. The largest branches of engineering are electrical, chemical, mechanical, and civil. Electrical engineers, for example, design communication tools, power plants, and computers. Chemical engineers deal with the production of chemicals for businesses. Mechanical engineers often focus on machines such as engines and pumps. Civil engineers design and build structures for public use.

WHAT IS CIVIL ENGINEERING?

Civil engineering is one of the oldest fields of engineering. As long as there have been people, there has been a need for structures that help them live in their communities and environments.

There are several kinds of civil engineering. Structural engineers make sure structures can stand up to forces such as hurricanes and earthquakes. Architectural engineers often design the insides of

Geotechnical engineers use computerized tools to locate and study different kinds of rocks.

Engineers talk at a dam in Mexico. The dam's power station creates electricity from running water.

THINK ABOUT IT

How might the different kinds of civil engineers described on these pages work together on one project?

buildings. Construction engineers plan for the materials and processes that will be used to create structures, while geotechnical engineers determine if it is safe to build structures. Water resource engineers handle water solutions, such as how to get water to people and how to keep it clean. Transportation engineers design highways and transportation systems for safe traffic flow.

EARLY CIVIL ENGINEERING

Well-built structures can last thousands of years after their construction. The Egyptian pyramids, which served as tombs for royalty, were some of the earliest civil engineering projects. The most famous of these pyramids—the pyramids of Giza—were built more than 4,500 years ago.

Like the pyramids, the Great Wall of China is a world wonder that people can still visit. The ancient Chinese

One of the Seven Wonders of the World, the pyramids of Giza are an engineering marvel.

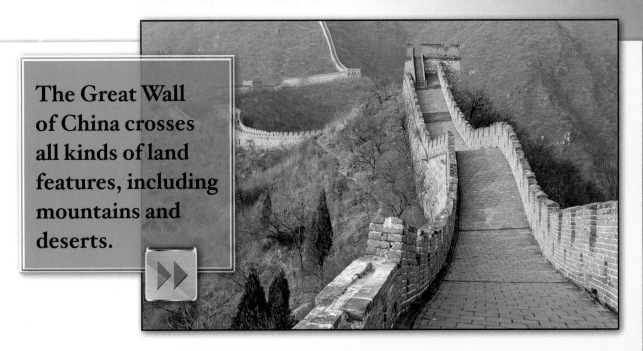

The Great Wall of China crosses all kinds of land features, including mountains and deserts.

began building the wall around 600 BCE to protect against invading armies. It grew to become more than 4,000 miles (6,500 kilometers) long.

There are even examples of early water resource engineering in history. From 312 BCE to 226 CE, the ancient Romans constructed a system of 11 **aqueducts** to bring water to Rome. The system, which used both bridges and underground pipes, is still partly used.

An **aqueduct** is a waterway that carries water from a source.

Working with Water

The ancient Romans created aqueducts because they needed to carry water to their communities. Not only did they want water for drinking and bathing, they needed it to irrigate crops. In other places, early versions of civil engineers built canals, or human-made waterways, to provide water to communities. Canals have been used for shipping, travel, and irrigation for more than 5,000 years.

This aqueduct is located in Segovia, Spain. It is one of the best-preserved Roman aqueducts and is still in use.

Modern water supply systems called waterworks collect, deliver, purify, store, and distribute water. They are made up of a pumping station and a water treatment system. Instead of gravity, pumps are used to transport water to places. The water is carried underground in large pipes, or mains, to all parts of a city or town.

Just as important as getting water to a community is taking dirty water—and waste—away.

New York City's High Bridge opened as an aqueduct in 1848. It is now used as a footbridge.

COMPARE AND CONTRAST

Some people live near oceans or seas instead of freshwater sources. Salt water must be specially treated before it can be used. Why do you think this is?

This photograph shows an ancient Roman sewer beneath the Roman Forum, a central meeting place in the city of Rome.

Although some ancient peoples, such as the Greeks, had sewers, truly effective sewage systems were not developed until the 1900s. Before this, some sewers mixed sewage with the water supply. This quickly spread illness and disease throughout a community.

Sewage systems collect wastewater and treat it before releasing it back into the environment. These

This California water plant treats wastewater and sends the clean water back to its source.

systems are made up of networks of underground sewers that carry the sewage through the treatment process to the point of removal. There are many ways of treating wastewater, including filters, bacteria, and chemicals. Sewage systems also handle the flow of rainwater, either separately or as part of a single system.

Sewage is any waste matter that is carried away by sewers, which are underground pipes or drains.

To Get to the Other Side

A bridge is any structure that allows people and vehicles to cross over an open space. Bridges span, or stretch across, deep pits in the earth, bodies of water, and roads. Engineers construct different kinds of bridges, depending on what is needed for the space to be crossed. Some types of bridges are fixed, while others are movable. Some open upward to allow ships to pass underneath. Others turn sideways.

Engineers have to think about certain natural forces

The Navajo Bridges span a part of the Grand Canyon in northern Arizona.

14

COMPARE AND CONTRAST

How are tension and compression different? How are they both important to bridge construction?

that affect all bridges. Two such forces are tension and compression. Tension is the force that pulls things apart. Compression is the force that presses things together. Every bridge deals with these forces, especially as cars, trains, and people add weight to it. A well-built bridge spreads out these forces so that the bridge does not become weakened and fail.

The Tower Bridge in London, England, is designed to allow ships to pass under it.

The beam bridge is the simplest and most common type of bridge. It is a horizontal, or level, structure with a support on each end. Piers may hold up the bridge between the two ends. A truss bridge is similar to a beam bridge but uses a triangular framework of metal or wood bars to increase its strength. Cantilever bridges use beams that stretch toward each other, as well as a framework of many bars. An arch bridge uses an arch or many arches under the roadway for support.

On a suspension bridge, the roadway hangs from strong wires called cables. The main cables hang between two or more towers. Smaller cables hang down

Each kind of bridge addresses the different needs of different types of roadways.

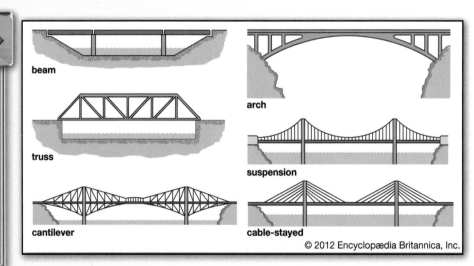

beam

truss

cantilever

arch

suspension

cable-stayed

© 2012 Encyclopædia Britannica, Inc.

from the main cables. A cable-stayed bridge also uses cables to support the roadway. However, its cables run directly between the towers and the roadway.

COMPARE AND CONTRAST

Suspension bridges span longer distances than any other type of bridge. Beam bridges often span the shortest distances. Why do you think this is?

The Golden Gate Bridge in northern California is a famous example of a suspension bridge.

THE PANAMA CANAL

The Panama Canal is a waterway connecting the Atlantic and Pacific oceans. It is about 50 miles (80 kilometers) long. Before it was built, ships traveling between the east and west coasts of North America had to go all the way around South America. The canal shortened the trip by about 9,200 miles (14,800 kilometers).

The Panama Canal cuts through a narrow piece of land between North and South America.

Building the canal was a huge job. It took about 10 years and more than 40,000 workers. More than

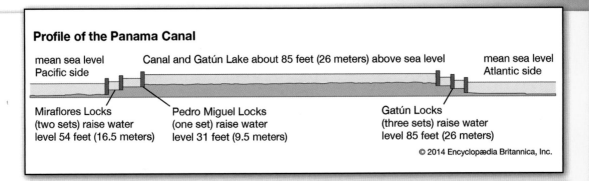

Profile of the Panama Canal

mean sea level
Pacific side

Canal and Gatún Lake about 85 feet (26 meters) above sea level

mean sea level
Atlantic side

Miraflores Locks
(two sets) raise water
level 54 feet (16.5 meters)

Pedro Miguel Locks
(one set) raise water
level 31 feet (9.5 meters)

Gatún Locks
(three sets) raise water
level 85 feet (26 meters)

© 2014 Encyclopædia Britannica, Inc.

This image shows why locks are needed to raise and lower ships passing through the canal.

60 million pounds (27 million kilograms) of dynamite was used to clear the land. The canal finally opened on August 15, 1914. About 14,000 ships use it each year. The American Society of Civil Engineers named the Panama Canal one of the Seven Modern Wonders of the World.

THINK ABOUT IT

Parts of the Panama Canal are at different heights above sea level. Gated sections called locks raise and lower ships so they can pass from one water level to another. What might happen if there were no locks?

THE HOOVER DAM

In the early 1900s, the southwestern United States needed a controlled water supply. The area often experienced flooding and droughts that made farming difficult. Civil engineers came up with a solution. They built a dam on the Colorado River at the border between Arizona and Nevada. With the dam, engineers can control the flow of the river's water.

The Hoover Dam was constructed between 1931 and 1936. It was a dangerous job with people working in extreme heat and at extreme

A view from the sky shows the Hoover Dam and the O'Callaghan-Tillman Bridge behind it.

THINK ABOUT IT

The Hoover Dam created Lake Mead, one of the largest human-made lakes in the world. How do you think this helps the people of the area?

heights. The dam is 726 feet (221 meters) high and 1,244 feet (380 meters) long at the crest. It is 660 feet (201 meters) thick at the bottom. It provides water as well as hydroelectric power to about 1.3 million people today.

This 1935 photo, taken as the Hoover Dam neared completion, shows the massive scope of the project.

THE CHANNEL TUNNEL

Between the countries of England and France lies a narrow body of water called the English Channel. For years, engineers wondered how to connect the two countries. Rather than build a very long bridge, they decided to construct a tunnel. Construction on the Channel Tunnel, sometimes called the Chunnel, began in 1987. It was officially opened on May 6, 1994.

This is an inside view of one of the tubes of the Channel Tunnel, as photographed in France.

THINK ABOUT IT

Engineers placed valves in the Chunnel walls to release air pressure caused by the super-fast trains. What might happen if there were no valves?

The tunnel is 31 miles (50 kilometers) long. It is actually three tunnels: two for rail traffic and one for services and security. Trains travel through the tunnel as fast as 100 miles (160 kilometers) per hour, and the trip takes about 35 minutes. In 2014, about 21 million passengers traveled through the Channel Tunnel.

Construction of this section took place 130 feet (40 meters) under the English Channel.

A New Engineering Marvel

Even today, civil engineers are creating structures the whole world holds in awe. Burj Khalifa is the name of the tallest building in the world. It reaches a height of 2,717 feet (828 meters). Opened in 2010, the building is located in the city of Dubai in the United Arab Emirates. Its design uses a series of "wings" off the central

Burj Khalifa soars over neighboring buildings. "Burj" means tower in Arabic.

tower, each with a concrete core to protect the higher floors from the effects of powerful winds.

Besides being the world's tallest building, Burj Khalifa holds the records for tallest freestanding structure, highest occupied floor, and highest outdoor observation deck, which is found on the 148th floor.

One World Trade Center, completed in 2013, is the tallest skyscraper in the Western Hemisphere.

WANTED: CIVIL ENGINEERS

As long as there are people in the world, civil engineers will be needed. Just as ancient civilizations required civil engineering, so will future civilizations. If the structures and processes in this resource are interesting to you, think about preparing for a career in civil engineering. First, work hard in math and science classes in both elementary and high school. Next, engineers must have at least a college bachelor's degree. Some civil engineers then continue to study and earn a master's degree.

Engineers talk over design and construction plans inside a tunnel of a suspension bridge.

In the United States, civil engineers must have a license. The first step to earning a license is to pass the Fundamentals of Engineering examination. After that, four years of training and work with licensed civil engineers is required. The final step is to pass the Principles and Practices of Engineering exam.

THINK ABOUT IT

Engineers often need to know about several kinds of engineering to complete a project successfully. Why do you think this is?

Engineers may do work behind the scenes of a project or take part in on-site construction.

27

ENGINEERING in ACTION

Build a Beam Bridge

The beam bridge is one of the oldest bridge designs. The weight of the horizontal beam pushes straight down on its supports and piers. The farther apart its piers, the weaker the beam becomes. This is why a beam bridge is usually used only to span distances of 250 feet (76 meters) or less.

Make your own beam bridge and watch the forces at work. Place equal-sized wood blocks or other objects to serve as supports

Engineers use models to test their ideas—just like you will with this project.

for either side of the bridge. Use an index card as your horizontal beam—your roadway. Then, stack weights, such as pennies, in the middle of the index card.

What happens when too much weight is stacked on the card? What can you do to provide more support? How would a civil engineer use a model such as this to design a bridge?

Next time you cross a bridge, think like an engineer and imagine the forces at work!

GLOSSARY

civilization A large group of people who share advanced ways of living and working.

crest The highest part or point of something.

distribute To spread out so as to cover something.

drought A long period of time during which there is very little or no rain.

dynamite A powerful explosive.

environment All the physical surroundings on Earth.

filter A device that is used to remove something unwanted from a liquid or gas that passes through it.

foundation The support upon which something rests.

freestanding Standing alone without being attached or supported by something else.

hydroelectric Relating to the production of electricity by using machines powered by moving water.

irrigate To supply with water by using human-made means, such as pipes.

license A permission granted by an authority to do something.

pump A device that moves liquids, especially by suction or pressure or both.

purify To remove dirty or harmful substances from something.

pyramid A very large structure that has a square base and four triangular sides that slope upward and meet at a point at the top.

valve A mechanical device that controls the flow of liquid or gas by opening and closing.

For More Information

Books

Brasch, Nicolas. *Amazing Built Structures*. Mankato, MN: Smart Apple Media, 2011.

Carmichael, L. E. *Amazing Feats of Civil Engineering*. Minneapolis, MN: Essential Library, 2015.

Ebner, Aviva. *Engineering Science Experiments*. New York, NY: Chelsea House, 2011.

Gonzales, Doreen. *What Are the 7 Wonders of the Modern World?* Berkeley Heights, NJ: Enslow Publishers, 2013.

Solway, Andrew. *Civil Engineering and the Science of Structures*. New York, NY: Crabtree Publishing Company, 2013.

Websites

Because of the changing nature of Internet links, Rosen Publishing has developed an online list of websites related to the subject of this book. This site is updated regularly. Please use this link to access the list:

http://www.rosenlinks.com/LFO/Civil

INDEX